DATE DUE	
	MAR 17 2013	
	JUN 02 2013	
	JUL 22 2013	

The Urbana Free Library

To renew: call 217-367-4057
or go to "*urbanafreelibrary.org*"
and select "Renew/Request Items"

Learn With Animals/
Aprende con los animales

Counting With Animals/

Cuenta con los animales

Sebastiano Ranchetti

Reading consultant: Susan Nations, M.Ed.,
author/literacy coach/consultant
in literacy development/

Consultora de lectura: Susan Nations, M.Ed.,
autora/tutora de lectoescritura/
consultora de desarrollo de lectoescritura

WEEKLY READER®
PUBLISHING

1

one monkey
- - - - - - - - - - - - - - -
un mono

3

4

2
two
flamingos
----
dos
flamencos

5

3
three frogs
----
tres ranas

7

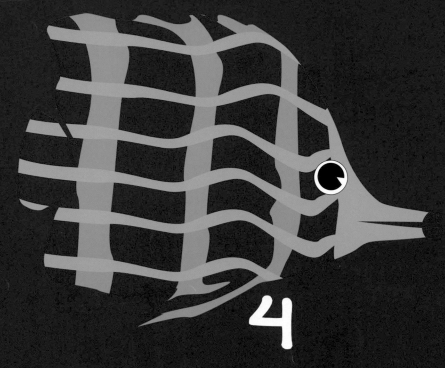

4

four fishes
----
cuatro peces

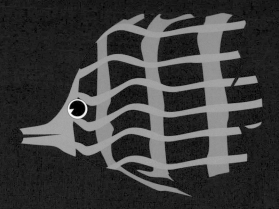
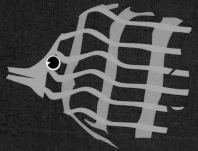
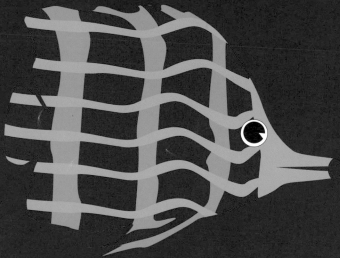

9

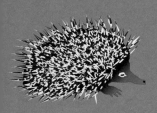

10

5
five
porcupines

- - - - - - - - - - - - - - - - -

cinco
puercoespines

6

six ladybugs
----
seis catarinas

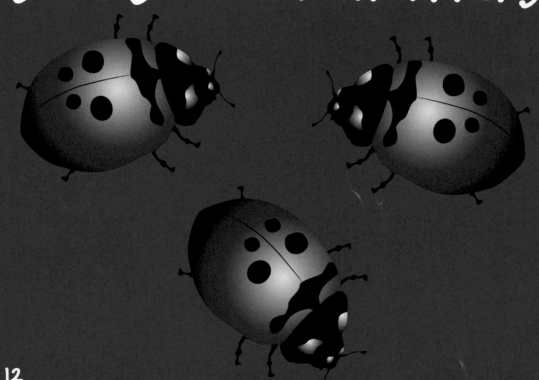

13

14

7
seven
salamanders
----
siete
salamandras

8

eight roosters
- -
ocho gallos

17

18

9
nine fishes
- - - - - - - - - - - - - - - -
nueve peces

19

10
ten penguins
----
diez pingüinos

21

1
<u>one</u>
uno

2
<u>two</u>
dos

3
<u>three</u>
tres

7
<u>seven</u>
siete

8
<u>eight</u>
ocho

4
four
cuatro

5
five
cinco

6
six
seis

9
nine
nueve

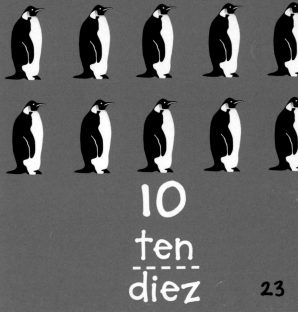

10
ten
diez

Please visit our web site at www.garethstevens.com.
For a free color catalog describing our list of high-quality books,
call 1-800-542-2595 (USA) or 1-800-387-3178 (Canada). Our fax: 877-542-2596

Library of Congress Cataloging-in-Publication Data

Ranchetti, Sebastiano.
   [Conta gli animali. Spanish & English]
   Counting with animals / by Sebastiano Ranchetti = Cuenta con los animales / por
Sebastiano Ranchetti — North American ed.
     p. cm. — (Learn with animals = Aprende con los animales)
   ISBN-10: 0-8368-9039-6   ISBN-13: 978-0-8368-9039-6 (lib. bdg. : alk. paper)
   ISBN-10: 0-8368-9044-2   ISBN-13: 978-0-8368-9044-0 (pbk. : alk. paper)
   1. Counting—Juvenile literature. I. Title. II. Title: Cuenta con los animales.
QA113.R35618   2008
513.2'11—dc22   2007042513

This North American edition first published in 2008 by
Weekly Reader® Books
An Imprint of Gareth Stevens Publishing
1 Reader's Digest Road
Pleasantville, NY 10570-7000 USA

This U.S. edition copyright © 2008 by Gareth Stevens, Inc. International Copyright © 2006 by Editoriale Jaca Book
spa, Milano, Italy. All rights reserved. First published in 2007 as *Conta gli animali* by Editoriale Jaca Book spa.

Gareth Stevens Senior Managing Editor: Lisa M. Guidone
Gareth Stevens Senior Editor: Barbara Bakowski
Gareth Stevens Creative Director: Lisa Donovan
Gareth Stevens Graphic Designer: Alexandria Davis
Spanish Translators: Tatiana Acosta and Guillermo Gutiérrez

Printed in the United States of America

1 2 3 4 5 6 7 8 9 10 09 08 07

About the AUTHOR and ARTIST

SEBASTIANO RANCHETTI has illustrated many books. He lives in the countryside near Florence, Italy.
His wife, three daughters, and some lively cats and dogs share his home. The ideas for his colorful
drawings come from nature and animals. He hopes his books spark your imagination!
Find out more at **www.animalsincolor.com**.

Información sobre el AUTOR/ARTISTA

SEBASTIANO RANCHETTI ha ilustrado muchos libros. Vive en el campo cerca de Florencia, Italia,
con su esposa, sus tres hijas y algunos traviesos gatos y perros. Sebastiano se inspira en
la naturaleza y los animales para sus coloridos dibujos, y espera que sus libros estimulen tu
imaginación. Para más información, visita **www.animalsincolor.com**.